What *REALLY* Happened
to the
DINOSAURS?

Copyright 1988 by Mark E. Dinsmore
and Creation-Life Publishers, Inc.

First Printing December, 1988

MASTER BOOKS
A division of CLP, Inc.
P.O. Box 1606
El Cajon, CA 92022

Library of Congress Cataloging-in-Publication Data

Dinsmore, Mark Eugene, 1964-
Chong, Jonathan, 1956-
 What Really Happened to the Dinosaurs?
 1. Dinosauria — juvenile literature.
 2. Paleontology.

 Printed in Hong Kong

ISBN 0-89051-142-X

To Mom and Dad

Thank you for teaching me
to use my head to think creatively,
my hands to build constructively,
and my heart to discern more critically,
so that I may share with others
the Truth of God's Word
and His Love.

Mark Dinsmore, **Author**

**To my American Mother,
Mrs. Clara Deyo**

I appreciate you all the days of my Life.

Jonathan Chong, **Illustrator**

5

WELCOME to the Institute for Creation Research — "ICR" for short. My name is Tracker John, and this is Dino Junior, my pet pet psittacosaurus (sih-TAK-uh-SAWR-us). You can just call him "D.J."

Here in the ICR building, scientists are learning more every day about how God made the world and everything in it. That includes the plants and animals, you and me, and even the DINOSAURS! Some were even like D.J. here, only bigger!

PART 1
IN THE BEGINNING

GOD made many different kinds of animals when he formed the earth and put life on it. He made them in all sorts of sizes, shapes and colors. But many kinds of animals are not alive today. All of some kinds of animals have died. One large group of animals that we call "dinosaurs" has mysteriously disappeared. Scientists have guessed at many reasons why the dinosaurs are gone, but maybe we can solve the mystery for ourselves simply by looking at the evidence.

Just like when your muddy footprints on the kitchen floor tell your mother that you visited the cookie jar, she knows from the footprint-evidence who took cookies!

There probably haven't been any dinosaurs making tracks in your kitchen, but they have made tracks in the ground that we can still see today. Let's go inside the ICR museum and see what *REALLY* happened to the dinosaurs!

DINOSAURS WERE called "terrible lizards" because some of the first people who found their huge fossil bones believed that they belonged to a family of giant lizards who were so strong that they "ruled" the earth. Some people still believe this way, and have made up an imaginary "prehistoric" time called the "Age of the Reptiles."

Do you think that the whole world used to be ruled by a bunch of lizards? We know that this is not true. God tells us that He made man so that he could rule the earth and take good care of it.

We cannot tell exactly what the many kinds of dinosaurs really looked like, but we can put animal skeletons back together just like a puzzle to get an idea of their size and shape. The puzzle pieces, called **fossils,** are buried and hidden in hard rock layers all over the earth. These layers used to be soft when they were first formed. Would you like to put together a dinosaur fossil puzzle?

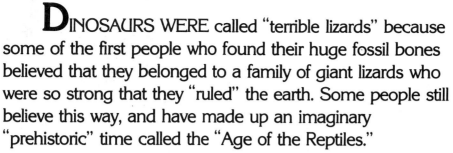

10

We can also learn about dinosaurs from the Bible. Did you know that people and dinosaurs used to live together at the same time? We know they did because God made both man and dinosaurs on the sixth day at the beginning of the world. This makes dinosaurs part of history, because they lived during the same time as our relatives.

11

DID YOU KNOW that you had relatives alive when God first made the world and everything in it? Adam and Eve were the first man and the first woman. They were specially made by God. Noah was a relative of Adam and Eve, and we are related to Noah. That makes us part of Adam and Eve's family too!

Adam and Eve, and Noah too, could have seen dinosaurs and other animals right in their own back yard! What do you think it would have been like to have a real live dinosaur for your neighbor?

I MENTIONED BEFORE that we can learn about dinosaurs from the Bible, but did you know that one of God's favorite animals was a Dinosaur? God calls this wonderful creature "BEHEMOTH," which means "huge and powerful." We can see why, from reading God's description in Job Chapter 40.

Behemoth eats grass like an ox. He has powerful hind legs and a strong belly. His tail is as big around as a large tree, and his bones are strong like metal. He finds his food in the mountain, and rests among reeds in the marsh under the shade of green plants. When the river floods, Behemoth is not bothered at all. No one can capture him when he is on guard, and he cannot be tamed.

WHAT KIND OF dinosaur does this sound like to you? According to my *Dinosaur Field Guide,* one creature we call Apatosaurus seems to fit this description pretty well. Can you picture an animal twice as tall and just as long as this building? That's how big an Apatosaurus was! God made these huge, strong animals to remind us of His own greatness and power.

15

PART 2
HOW SIN CHANGED THE WORLD

AT THE very beginning when God made everything, dinosaurs were just as friendly as D.J. But our first relatives, Adam and Eve, disobeyed God. Their disobedience was the first sin. When sin came into the world, some dinosaurs and other animals changed.

IN THE BEGINNING when God made the earth, everything was just right — not too hot and not too cold. God made the earth a perfect place for plants and animals to grow and for people to live. The world was just like God had planned, and He tells us that it was very good.

18

The flowers and trees God made grew to be very, very large. So did all of the insects, animals, and dinosaurs. This was a time of giants.

Green plants covered the earth and made terrific food! Underground springs watered the soil (Genesis 2:6), making the entire earth moist and rich. It was a beautiful world.

19

BUT SOON, all the people who lived in this amazing world hated God. All except one man and his family. That man was Noah. Noah told the people about God and how He had made the earth, but the people would not listen. They just laughed at him.

20

God told Noah that He was going to destroy the whole world with a flood. This flood was sent by God to judge the evil, violent world. Only the good man Noah, his family, and the animals that God brought into the Ark were saved.

21

NOAH'S ARK was not a small boat. There was plenty of room for everyone and lots of space left over for food and storage on Noah's huge cargo ship. It was very, very big — bigger than your house or even a big barn. It was as tall as a four story building, and longer than a football field. Now that is pretty big, isn't it!

At least two of every kind of dinosaur and every other kind of animal went on the Ark with Noah and his family. The larger animals could be taken on board while they were still babies. Some full-grown dinosaurs were even as small as a chicken. That's just about D.J.'s size!

AFTER GOD had closed the door to the Ark, the Flood came. The ground shook terribly and the earth was broken open in many places. Volcanoes of red-hot, melted rock gushed out of cracks in the ground for the first time. Huge underground springs of water burst open and spilled out over the earth. It was a horrible, terrible thing to happen to such a beautiful place. All because the people didn't listen to God.

All of the water above the earth fell down to the ground. The Bible tells us that this was the very first time it had rained on the earth. It rained very hard for 40 days and 40 nights. It rained so hard that all of the ground and all of the cities the people had built began to fall apart and wash away.

The sky became completely black, even during the daytime, and the thunder and lightning probably never stopped while it rained. The whole world was covered by rushing, swirling water and violent storms. Hurricanes and tornadoes kept stirring things up like a big blender until all of God's original creation was washed away and buried miles deep in tons and tons of mud!

Have you ever been in a terrible storm before? You can be glad that you were not in this storm, because nothing outside the Ark survived. Noah's Flood was the worst storm that ever was, but God kept Noah and his family and all the different kinds of animals safe on the Ark. God had designed the Ark for Noah so that it would not sink.

25

PART 3
DINOSAURS AFTER THE FLOOD

EVEN THOUGH the Ark would not sink, Noah and his family may have been pretty seasick after being tossed up and down and around and around by the huge waves of the great Flood ocean. How would you like to be stuck on a roller coaster that didn't stop, day or night, for over one year? That is how long Noah and his family were on board the Ark with all the animals. They were probably very glad when the Ark finally landed on Mt. Ararat!

Several days after they had landed, Noah and his family left the Ark. All of the animals came out also, and some began to have babies. Soon the world began to fill again with animals and people. But the earth was no longer a beautiful place to live in. All of the great forests were gone. All of the huge green plants and colorful flowers were gone. There was only dried mud. And rocks. And more mud and more rocks.

27

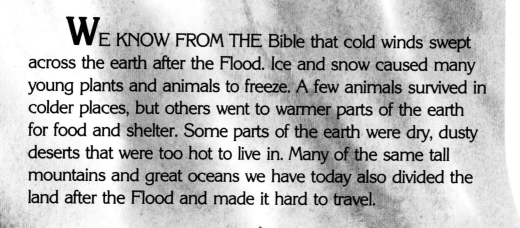

WE KNOW FROM THE Bible that cold winds swept across the earth after the Flood. Ice and snow caused many young plants and animals to freeze. A few animals survived in colder places, but others went to warmer parts of the earth for food and shelter. Some parts of the earth were dry, dusty deserts that were too hot to live in. Many of the same tall mountains and great oceans we have today also divided the land after the Flood and made it hard to travel.

Many of the dinosaurs died because the plants they ate for food were not able to grow as before. Some plants were not able to grow at all. Fresh water and moist jungles were harder to find. Some of the flying animals, such as pterodactyls (TER-o- DAK-tils) and pteranodons (ter-AN-o-dons), may have been too heavy to fly in the new sky because the air was much thinner.

Because the air was different after the Flood, the very large dinosaurs may not have been able to breathe enough to stay alive very long. They needed oxygen just like we do, but we don't need nearly as much as they did!

28

There may also be other reasons why dinosaurs are hard to find today. The plant-eating dinosaurs would have been very difficult to keep out of gardens that people planted for food. Farmers might have built huge walls around their houses and gardens to keep the dinosaurs out. They may have also dug large pits for the animals to fall into. The farmers trapped the animals for a good reason, though: Finding a bug in your lunch might ruin your day, but finding a dinosaur in your garden could ruin your whole year. A single plant-eating dinosaur like Apatosaurus could have eaten 2000 pounds of broccoli, carrots, corn, peas, beans and lettuce IN ONE DAY! Even if you liked all of those vegetables, how long do you think it would take YOU to eat a one-ton salad?

Shepherds and ranchers may have also hunted dinosaurs to protect their flocks and herds of livestock animals. There are many stories about how brave men hunted and killed very large animals like the dinosaurs, not very long ago.

29

Now that you know what *REALLY* happened to the dinosaurs, you can be a "dinosaur tracker" too. After all, they might not all be gone! You will not find one in your back yard like Noah could have, but there are scientists who believe that some dinosaurs are alive today, deep in the dark jungles of Africa.

I am going on another dinosaur adventure there soon. If you come with me and look very hard, you might be able to bring back one of your very own, just like D.J.!

Would you like to go on another great dinosaur adventure with me soon?